YOUR KNOWLEDGE HAS VALUE

- We will publish your bachelor's and master's thesis, essays and papers

- Your own eBook and book - sold worldwide in all relevant shops

- Earn money with each sale

Upload your text at www.GRIN.com and publish for free

Video Games For The Elderly

How can video games be made more appealing to the elderly?

Christian Dordel

Bibliographic information published by the German National Library:

The German National Library lists this publication in the National Bibliography; detailed bibliographic data are available on the Internet at http://dnb.dnb.de.

ISBN: 9783346983169
This book is also available as an ebook.

© GRIN Publishing GmbH
Trappentreustraße 1
80339 München

All rights reserved

Print and binding: Books on Demand GmbH, Norderstedt, Germany
Printed on acid-free paper from responsible sources.

The present work has been carefully prepared. Nevertheless, authors and publishers do not incur liability for the correctness of information, notes, links and advice as well as any printing errors.

GRIN web shop: https://www.grin.com/document/1430699

Video Games For The Elderly

How can video games be made more appealing to the elderly?

(Videospiele für Senioren)

Seminararbeit

am Lehrstuhl für Betriebswirtschaftslehre,
insb. Gestaltung soziotechnischer Informationssysteme

im Studiengang Master Wirtschaftswissenschaft

von Christian Dordel

Sommersemester 2023

Contents

List of Figures

1 Introduction

The group of the elderly is formed by all people aged 65 and over (Orimo et al., 2006), and their percentage of the total population is continuously growing (United Nations, 2020). According to the United Nations (2020) report on world population aging, the share of the elderly has increased over the past 30 years from 6 percent in 1990 to 9 percent in 2019, and is projected to further increase over the next 30 years to approximately 16 percent by the year 2050. A steady increase in life expectancy and a decline in birth rate are the reasons identified by the United Nations (2020) and WHO World Health Organization (2015).

With increasing age, people are affected by impairments and disabilities, and in contrast to other age groups, the elderly are at higher risk for age-related losses in hearing, vision, mobility, and cognition (Lukaitis & Davey, 2012; Palacio et al., 2017; WHO World Health Organization, 2015). To address these psychological and physical declines, video games are being used in a non-gaming context for therapeutic treatments, and a significant amount of research is focused on how video games can improve physical and psychological abilities of the elderly (Bleakley et al., 2015; Y.-L. Wang et al., 2020).

Playing video games is in general a leisure activity (Cota et al., 2015) that is primarily preferred by younger people (Ijsselsteijn et al., 2007). The growing group of the elderly and their hesitation to play video games for entertainment, becomes a potential target group for the video game industry (Derboven et al., 2012). Because age groups are heterogeneous in their demands towards content and operation of video games (Ijsselsteijn et al., 2007), the industry would need to publish playable and attractive games for the elderly to obtain their attention. Nap et al. (2009) and Y.-L. Wang et al. (2020) have identified that there is limited research existing on elderly people playing video games for entertainment purposes, therefore further research is required to close this gap.

To provide a guideline in order to achieve attractiveness and usability of video games for people aged 65 and older, this paper is guided by following research question:

How can video games be made more appealing to the elderly?

The Design Science Research Methodology introduced by Walls et al. (1992) and further refined by Hevner et al. (2004) and Peffers et al. (2007) will be used to address this question. Existing knowledge and theories will be applied on requirements for improvement of video games, resulting in the creation of an artifact (Walls et al., 1992). The artifact is intended to solve the initial problem and becomes itself a part of the knowledge base (Peffers et al., 2007). This research is described in detail in the remainder of this paper.

The structure of this paper is aligned to recommended publication scheme by Gregor and Hevner (2013, p. 350) with minor adjustments. The current section *introduction*, defines the problem, shows significance for research, and specifies the research question. This is followed by the second section with *literature review* to gather relevant research and theories related to the research question of this paper. In the third section, the applicable design science research *methodology* is explained in detail. The steps for creating the artifact are processed within the fourth section *design*. The fifth and final section will close with *discussion* and covers the conclusions drawn from this research.

2 Literature Review

This section has two objectives: first, to identify similar research that corresponds to the research question of this paper, and second, to gather kernel theories and artifacts including constructs, models, methods, or instantiations, that serve as a knowledge base to design a new artifact as a research result of this paper.

Existing research on video games associated with elderly people is focused primarily on medical and therapeutic benefits in the treatment of disease (Bleakley et al., 2015; L. V. Costa et al., 2018; Gamberini et al., 2008; J.-Y. Wang, 2014). Allaire et al. (2013) emphasize that playing video games improves the cognitive abilities of the elderly people and Derboven et al. (2012) identify that well-being benefits from social interaction by playing. Nguyen et al. (2017), Chua et al. (2013), and L. Costa and Veloso (2016) recommend intergenerational gaming to increase interaction between age groups in order to improve their relationship and mutual understanding.

There are existing two research papers that focus on the design of video games with entertainment purpose for the elderly, the first by Cota et al. (2015) and the second by Vasconcelos et al. (2012).
The study by Cota et al. (2015) shows the development and demonstration of a smartphone based video game to a group of elderly people. The objectives are to identify the preferred game genres, to verify the usability of a specific designed game, and to determine the factors that motivate the elderly to play video games (Cota et al., 2015).

Vasconcelos et al. (2012) designed a gaming platform with a set of games to be played with a tablet. The research had been processed by literature review, observations, questionnaires, and game development through iterative prototyping, resulting in the identification of 10 game design guidelines for validation in future research (Vasconcelos et al., 2012).

Additional research on the motivation to play and preferences of the elderly has been published by Ijsselsteijn et al. (2007) and Nap et al. (2009), but without developing a game or prototype. Boot et al. (2018) study the gaming behavior of the elderly based on an experimental computer system with optional game play, to derive user preferences and habits, and Gerling et al. (2012) present a summary of recommendations for game design and assign validation to future research.

There are certain parallels in designing websites and video games for elderly users, because both use similar input and output devices (Czaja & Lee, 2012; Gerling et al., 2012), navigational and graphical elements correspond (Boot et al., 2018; Czaja & Lee, 2007), and the elderly have the same limitations in use because of their age-related impairments (Gerling et al., 2012). Research theories and artifacts by Castilla et al. (2016), Dickinson et al. (2005), Hanson and Crayne (2005), Lukaitis and Davey (2012), and Zaphiris et al. (2007) define guidelines for visualization and navigation, that are taken into account for this paper.

3 Methodology

In order to generate guidelines that answer the research question of this paper, the methodological approach used is Design Science by Hevner et al. (2004) and Peffers et al. (2007). Hevner et al. (2004) have developed a conceptual framework based on the design theory established by Walls et al. (1992). According to Hevner et al. (2004), design science is a problem solving process that receives input from two sources, first as requirements by business and environment, and second from applicable knowledge consisting of existing kernel theories. The result of this procedure are artifacts, which are defined as constructs, models, methods, or instantiations (Hevner et al., 2004). In a broader sense, an artifact can be any designed object that includes any research activity and knowledge of theory, to define the functionality and architecture of the solution (Peffers et al., 2007).

The design process described by Hevner et al. (2004), was adopted by Peffers et al. (2007) into a six-step Design Science Research Process Model, with the individual steps of (1) *problem identification and motivation*, (2) *define of the objectives for a solution*, (3) *design and development*, (4) *demonstration*, (5) *evaluation*, and (6) *communication*. These are discussed in more detail in this section and supplemented with applicable activities related to the research question of this paper.

Peffers et al. (2007) define the initial step *problem identification and motivation*, as the specification of the research problem in order to develop an appropriate artifact to solve this issue. Depending on the complexity, it might be necessary to divide the problem into smaller levels. The mentioned motivation signals the value that can be achieved by a solution, either for the researcher or for the audience of the research, and shows the importance for the solution (Peffers et al., 2007).

The problem and motivation regarding the research question of this paper have already been covered in the first and second sections. The age group of elderly people is continuously growing, the average life expectancy is increasing, and because of age-related impairments (United Nations, 2020; WHO World Health Organization, 2015), this group has individual interests in spending their leisure time with their own specific demands towards video games (Ijsselsteijn et al., 2007; Nap et al., 2009).

Define of the objectives for a solution is the second step in this process sequence by Peffers et al. (2007), in order to create the first artifact at all to solve this problem, or to derive the improvement that a new artifact will have over an existing solution. The former is a qualitative description of the expected support, while the latter would be a quantitative comparison between the existing and the new solution. This implies a clear knowledge of the state of problems and their solutions (Peffers et al., 2007).

The objective of the artifact resulting of this paper, is to develop a solution to make video games more appealing to the elderly. A theory-driven approach is followed by specifying meta-requirements based on the literature review, which is demonstrated in the fourth section of this paper.

As third step, that contains the creation of the artifact, Peffers et al. (2007) declare *design and development* in their process model.

The fourth section of this paper is dedicated to the design step, therein the design principles are derived from existing artifacts and kernel theories, and decisions are made about the design features that the newly created artifact should cover (Meth et al., 2015; Peffers et al., 2007). The final development of this artifact is beyond the scope of this paper and will therefore not be discussed in detail, but it would consist of creating samples with short video game sequences and additional visual and audio simulations.

Demonstration of the use of the created artifact is the fourth step defined by Peffers et al. (2007) and this can be performed, for example, by simulations, studies, or experiments.

The previously theoretically created samples and game simulations would be presented to a test group in a controlled experiment (Hevner et al., 2004) to obtain subjective feedback by interviews or questionnaires on ease of use and usability, and in addition the participants are observed by researchers to collect objective data. Because of the omitted development, the demonstration and the following steps are not processed within the scope of this paper.

With *evaluation* as step five, Peffers et al. (2007) compare the results of demonstrating the artifact with the previously defined objectives of a solution outlined in step two. Methods of evaluation are depending on the artifact, for example by performance measures, satisfaction surveys, simulations, client feedback, or objective comparison of quantifiable performance measures. As result of the evaluation, a decision is taken whether to proceed to the next step in this process model, or to go back to step three in order to redesign and improve the artifact, or further back to step two for refinement of the meta-requirements (Peffers et al., 2007).

If evaluation would be processed within this research, then feedback and observations of the demonstration phase are evaluated against the meta-requirements defined. The aggregated results then determine if the created artifact meets the requirements, or if the iterative process needs to be initiated with a loop back to step two for review of literature and theory, or back to step three to start a redesign of the artifact.

Peffers et al. (2007) define *communication* as the sixth and final step in their process model. The identified problem with its artifact as a solution needs to be communicated to researchers and other relevant audiences (Peffers et al., 2007) by reporting in scientific and professional publications, and through professional events that will reach the target audience (Hevner et al., 2004).

The finalized artifact along with the identified problem of this paper, are supposed to be published in scientific journals to motivate other researchers to continue and expand research in this professional section. The game industry should be made aware of observations that have been made in this specific area of interest, in order to consider these for future game design. Furthermore, the created artifact will serve as an additional resource to the knowledge base (Hevner et al., 2004).

To summarize the Design Science Research Process Model graphically, Figure 1 provides an overview of each step, including the iterative cycle and the previously specified actions for this paper. The shaded steps indicate the process activities that are out of scope of this paper.

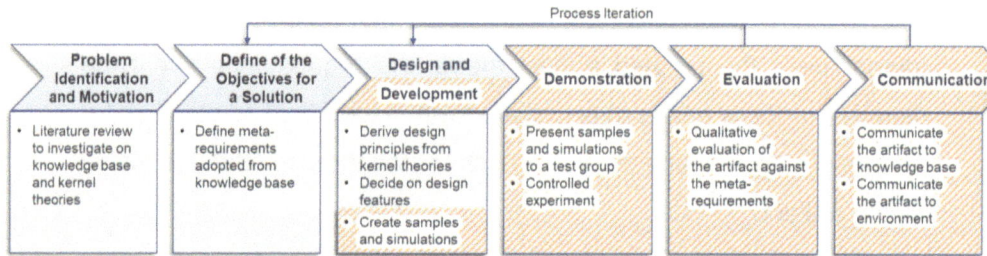

Figure 1. Design Science Research Process Model
(adapted from Peffers et al., 2007, p. 54)

4 Design

This section describes in detail the design process as initial part of the third step of Peffers et al.'s (2007) Design Science Research Process Model, as well as the definition of objectives for a solution of the second step. The results of the literature review in the second section are transferred into meta-requirements (Gregor & Hevner, 2013; Walls et al., 1992), which are demanding specific functionalities to be covered by the new artifact (Meth et al., 2015). Subsequently, these meta-requirements are mapped to design principles (Gregor & Hevner, 2013; Meth et al., 2015), which are called meta-design by Walls et al. (1992). These design principles are formulated at a higher level of abstraction and are based on knowledge derived from other research, theories, or artifacts (Gregor & Hevner, 2013), which are retrieved by the literature review. Finally, concrete design features are derived from the design principles, and these features are components that the created artifact needs to obtain (Meth et al., 2015).

4.1 Meta-Requirements

Based on the results of the literature review in the second section of this paper, within this subsection the meta-requirements are defined for the design of the artifact.

Research has shown that the elderly are not reluctant to use new technologies (Czaja & Lee, 2007; Ijsselsteijn et al., 2007), the prerequisite is that they are enabled to learn how to use these properly (Jochems et al., 2013). Further required is the technical expandability of the system with improvements, updates and new games

(Vasconcelos et al., 2012). This forms the first meta-requirement that the technical devices and equipment for playing games need to be easily operated and purchased.

MR01: Easy access to technology and to sourcing of equipment

Aging-related impairments have various impacts on different cognitive and physical abilities (WHO World Health Organization, 2015), where the former is discussed in this paragraph and the latter in the next meta-requirement. Cognitive limitations in processing speed and in handling of simultaneous or complex tasks are observed (Czaja & Lee, 2007; Li et al., 2001; Lukaitis & Davey, 2012; Salthouse, 1996). This is noticeable in reading and comprehension, because more time is needed to read difficult words or to understand long and complex sentences (Dickinson et al., 2005; Lukaitis & Davey, 2012; Palacio et al., 2017). Furthermore, a decrease in attention and memory is identified (Gerling et al., 2012; Zaphiris et al., 2007), resulting in an inability to focus on relevant information and being easily distracted (Hawthorn, 2000; Vasconcelos et al., 2012). As result of these described cognitive implications, the second meta-requirement summarizes these aspects and demands in order to avoid a cognitive overload for elderly people by playing video games.

MR02: Avoid cognitive overload

The physical decline mentioned in the previous paragraph manifests itself primarily in the areas of vision, hearing, and mobility (Palacio et al., 2017; Zaphiris et al., 2007). Loss of ability to see at close range, reduced field of vision, and decrease in clarity, color, and detail of vision are reported (Gerling et al., 2012; Hanson & Crayne, 2005; Lukaitis & Davey, 2012). Sounds at high frequency and speed are more often not recognized by the elderly people (Czaja & Lee, 2012; Zaphiris et al., 2007), and as a result, audio effects are not perceived by them (Gamberini et al., 2008). The reduced sensory and motor skills have a negative impact on the game control in relation to the equipment used for gaming (Gerling et al., 2012; Palacio et al., 2017; Vasconcelos et al., 2012). The third meta-requirement is derived regarding the consideration of physical and sensory impairments of elderly people in order to enable them to properly use video games.

MR03: Accessibility with physical or sensory disabilities

To be consistent with the previously described implications that derive the second and third meta-requirements, not all elderly people are affected by the same disabilities or to the same degree of impairment (Hawthorn, 2000; Ijsselsteijn et al., 2007). For this reason, it is necessary that each user will be able to make individual decisions about the required level of adaption of video games (Dickinson et al., 2005; Gamberini et al., 2008; Ijsselsteijn et al., 2007; Zaphiris et al., 2007). Therefore, a request for customization defines the fourth meta-requirement.

MR04: Customizable preferences and user settings

It is reasonable to assume that the process and structure of the game is a novice to the elderly user, even with trial and error, help will be necessary to accomplish the game control and reach the goal of the game (Hanson & Crayne, 2005; Zaphiris et al., 2007). Similar to an instruction manual, the elderly user requires support in playing video games, either to get properly started, or in situations where the user gets stuck during the game (Dickinson et al., 2005; Hanson & Crayne, 2005; Zaphiris et al., 2007). This formulates the fifth meta-requirement, which is the integration of an appropriate support functionality in the game.

MR05: In-game support functionality

Playing video games does not mean that elderly people are supposed to play alone and to be socially isolated (L. Costa & Veloso, 2016; Nguyen et al., 2017). According to Derboven et al. (2012) and Ijsselsteijn et al. (2007), people have more fun playing video games together with others, therefore users should have the opportunity to connect and interact with others while playing. This can be with people of the same age group or intergenerational with different age groups, for example as a family leisure activity (Chua et al., 2013; Nguyen et al., 2017). This demand for social inclusion is covered by the sixth meta-requirement.

MR06: Social inclusion of elderly people

Playing non-digital games is a leisure activity for many people, including the elderly (Vasconcelos et al., 2012), which is supposed to be fun and pleasure (Allaire et al., 2013; Cota et al., 2015; Nguyen et al., 2017). This forms the seventh meta-requirement that playing video games should provide at minimum the same pleasure to the elderly people than playing non-digital games.

MR07: Pleasure for elderly people by video games

To respond to age-related impairments and to allow elderly users to improve their physical and mental fitness (Bleakley et al., 2015; L. V. Costa et al., 2018; Gamberini et al., 2008), video games are supposed to include exercise and training components. There is evidence that these have a positive effect on the user (L. V. Costa et al., 2018; Zelinski & Reyes, 2009) and that the elderly are interested in these features (Whitlock et al., 2012). Allaire et al. (2013) outline that cognitive abilities can be improved and Nguyen et al. (2017) emphasize the positive physical effects. This defines the eighth and final meta-requirement to include exercise and training for health purposes.

MR08: Improve health

The following Figure 2 illustrates all eight previously defined meta-requirements.

Meta-Requirements

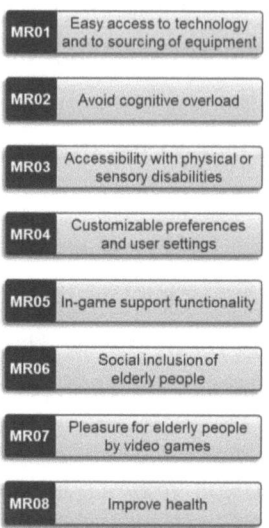

Figure 2. Meta-Requirements

4.2 Design Principles

Derived from the previously formulated eight meta-requirements, the corresponding design principles, which have their origin in the initial literature review, are described in this subsection.

The first design principle focuses on the technical system, with respect to the first meta-requirement. The selection from the variety of available hardware needs also to take the demands of the second and third meta-requirements into account, regarding impairments of the elderly. Boot et al. (2018), Cota et al. (2015), Czaja and Lee (2007), Gerling et al. (2012), Hanson and Crayne (2005), Nap et al. (2009), and Vasconcelos et al. (2012) provide the knowledge base for this design principle.

DP01: Technical implementation

The similarity between the second, third, fourth, and fifth meta-requirements, is the demand to accommodate to users' impairments and request for support in order to provide an appropriate game experience. Considering research of Czaja and Lee (2007), Dickinson et al. (2005), Gamberini et al. (2008), Gerling et al. (2012), Hanson and Crayne (2005), Ijsselsteijn et al. (2007), Lukaitis and Davey (2012), Salthouse (1996), Vasconcelos et al. (2012), and Zaphiris et al. (2007), the second design principle includes the knowledge base to provide comprehensibility and to support users mental and physical abilities.

DP02: Comprehension and support

To avoid social isolation of the elderly by including them in the interactions of other age groups, is addressed by the sixth meta-requirement. Chua et al. (2013), L. Costa and Veloso (2016), Derboven et al. (2012), Gerling et al. (2012), Nguyen et al. (2017), and Vasconcelos et al. (2012) support the third design principle with their artifacts.

DP03: Social interaction

The seventh meta-requirement is intended to provide an incentive in order to entertain the elderly users by playing games. Not for medical or therapeutic reasons, but for the elderly's enjoyment and to enrich their leisure time, the fourth design principle is supported with knowledge by Boot et al. (2018), Cota et al. (2015), Gerling et al. (2012), Ijsselsteijn et al. (2007), Nap et al. (2009), and Vasconcelos et al. (2012).

DP04: Entertainment

Improving of health status and preventing disease in elderly people is demanded by the eighth meta-requirement. Research by Allaire et al. (2013), Bleakley et al. (2015), L. V. Costa et al. (2018), Nguyen et al. (2017), and Vasconcelos et al. (2012) influence the fifth and final design principle, that takes disease prevention and the therapeutic aspect into account.

DP05: Medical prophylaxis and therapy

These five design principles and their relationship to the eight meta-requirements are illustrated in Figure 3.

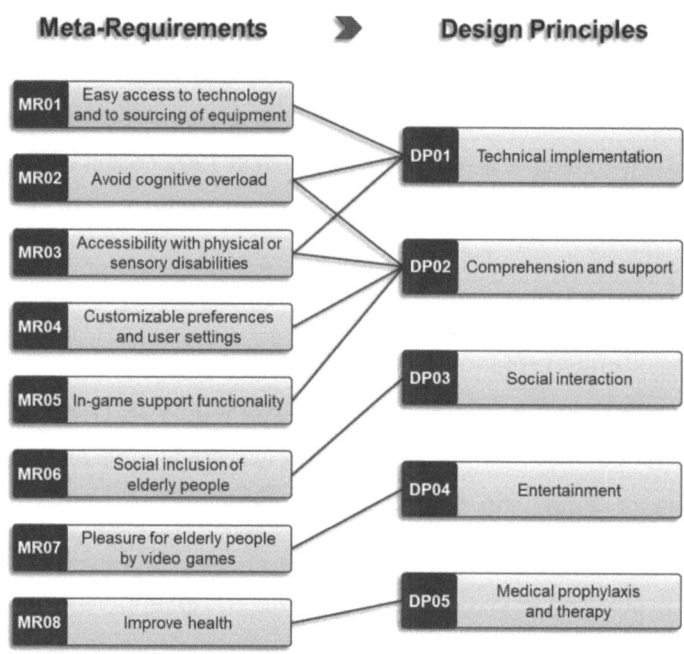

Figure 3. Meta-Requirements and Design Principles

4.3 Design Features

To design the artifact, concrete design features are derived from the previously defined design principles based on kernel theories, to comply with the demands of the meta-requirements.

From the first design principle regarding the *technical implementation*, the first design feature is concluded. It is decided to use a smartphone or a tablet as the technical device on which the video game is played, with a clear tendency towards the tablet. Both are operated using a touch screen as a direct input device, with the advantage that this is easier for the elderly to adopt and is a more natural method of interaction in contrast to holding a game controller or using a computer mouse, which both are more demanding in consideration of age-related limitations (Gerling et al., 2012; Jochems et al., 2013; Palacio et al., 2017). Smartphone and tablet, both can be updated via internet with software and new games, and in addition, both are portable, no additional hardware is required, and they can be operated in different positions that are comfortable for the user (Vasconcelos et al., 2012). In conclusion, the larger screen size favors the tablet over the smaller smartphone to compensate for the loss in vision (Vasconcelos et al., 2012).

DF01: Tablet as gaming device

The next nine design features are originated from the second design principle, which is based on the knowledge for *comprehension and support*. Beginning with the decline in vision, the second feature addresses the style and size, both of text, symbols, icons, and buttons.

The fonts used should be sans serif and at a larger scale that individual letters can be clearly distinguished, furthermore, symbols and icons need to have a larger size to be more easily seen by elderly users (Boot et al., 2018; Castilla et al., 2016; Dickinson et al., 2005; Zaphiris et al., 2007).

DF02: Style and size of fonts and objects

Continuing with vision, the third design feature addresses the use of colors and contrast at appropriate levels. The contrast between different colors and between background and text needs to be at a high level in order to distinguish the different information, but too many different colors will distract the user and the colors green and blue look similar when used in close proximity (Dickinson et al., 2005; Hawthorn, 2000; Vasconcelos et al., 2012; Zaphiris et al., 2007).

DF03: Colors and contrast

The fourth design feature addresses hearing impairment, to be countered with limited usage of sounds that accompany the actions during the game (Boot et al., 2018; Hawthorn, 2000). The sound in general needs to be at a lower frequency and spoken instructions should be avoided (Vasconcelos et al., 2012).

DF04: Sounds

To meet the cognitive decline and slower speed for processing of information, the graphical appearance is supposed to be simplified by the fifth design feature (Castilla et al., 2016; Czaja & Lee, 2007; Hawthorn, 2000). This means that the screen is not overloaded and all information and buttons have their consistent position (Dickinson et al., 2005) with sufficient space between each other (Ijsselsteijn et al., 2007).

DF05: Simplified graphical appearance

In addition to the mental state of the elderly, the complexity of the game and of textual information is reduced by the sixth design feature, by demanding a simple storyline (Boot et al., 2018; Cota et al., 2015; Vasconcelos et al., 2012), short game sequences, simple terminology, and short sentences (Czaja & Lee, 2007; Dickinson et al., 2005; Lukaitis & Davey, 2012; Palacio et al., 2017).

DF06: Complexity of storyline and text

Affected by decline in attention, elderly people are easily distracted during the game (Czaja & Lee, 2007), therefore the seventh design feature prevents of unnecessary distraction by in-game events and actions. Distractions to be omitted include, for example, playing against a time limit (Cota et al., 2015; J.-Y. Wang, 2014), performing multiple tasks simultaneously (Czaja & Lee, 2007; Gerling et al., 2012; Hawthorn, 2000), or the appearance of irrelevant cues and pop-up notifications (Czaja & Lee, 2007).

DF07: Distraction by in-game events

The eighth design feature takes care of the difficulty and speed of the game (Czaja & Lee, 2007; Gamberini et al., 2008), both at high levels require strong cognitive attention from the user, therefore these settings need to be adjustable.

DF08: Difficulty and speed

Elderly people might get stuck in a certain sequence during game play and need further assistance to able to continue playing, the ninth feature addresses the implementation of an in-game tutorial functionality to support the user with help and a strategy guide (Dickinson et al., 2005; Vasconcelos et al., 2012; Zaphiris et al., 2007).

DF09: Help and support function

In order to meet the different needs based on each user's individual health and comfort situation, the tenth design feature allows for setting of user preferences with personalized options, for example font size, colors, contrast, audio, zooming, and game difficulty and speed (Dickinson et al., 2005; Gamberini et al., 2008; Hanson & Crayne, 2005).

DF10: Set user preferences

The eleventh design feature is a conclusion of the second, third, and fourth design principles. The feature addresses the multilingualism, that enables users to read screen details or instructions in their own native language to reduce cognitive load and increase the user's enjoyment of the game (Nap et al., 2009; Zaphiris et al., 2007). This feature allows a connection with other users who speak other languages without any barriers. (Nap et al., 2009; Zaphiris et al., 2007).

DF11: Native language

Social interaction as the third and *entertainment* as the fourth design principle, both provide the decision for the twelfth design feature. An option for multiplayer mode will maintain or reinforce the social network of the elderly, allowing them to play locally or remotely with family, friends, or new people (Chua et al., 2013; L. Costa & Veloso, 2016; Derboven et al., 2012; Gerling et al., 2012; Nguyen et al., 2017). This enables the elderly to play with their grandchildren when they are unable to visit each other frequently, or to compete with friends (Gerling et al., 2012; Vasconcelos et al., 2012).

DF12: Multiplayer mode

The next three design features are based on the fourth design principle *entertainment*. Starting with the thirteenth feature, the elderly prefer video games that are originated from traditional, non-digital card games and board games they played in the past, because the elderly know the rules and are reminded of the time when they were young (Boot et al., 2018; Cota et al., 2015; Nap et al., 2009). Simplistic video games are preferred by the elderly, as long as the complexity of learning and operating the game is at a level appropriate to their abilities (Gerling et al., 2012; Nap et al., 2009).

DF13: Traditional and simple games

Continuing with the fourteenth design feature, users are motivated by the ability to compete with others or challenge themselves to reach the next level of the game (Cota et al., 2015; Derboven et al., 2012; Nap et al., 2009).

DF14: Competition and leaderboard

To conclude the *entertainment* principle with the fifteenth design feature, a variety of games need to be offered that users can choose their favorites and are not frustrated by having only one single game available (Cota et al., 2015; Vasconcelos et al., 2012).

DF15: Variety of games

The final sixteenth design feature is derived from the fifth design principle *medical prophylaxis and therapy*, and depends on the individual intention of the game. As a simple leisure activity, gaming enhances the cognitive abilities of the user, which can be further intensified with specific in-game training activities (Allaire et al., 2013; Whitlock et al., 2012). Certain game structures allow for physical exercising components (Bleakley et al., 2015; Derboven et al., 2012), but with regards to the selected gaming device this is optional and only the cognitive effect is taken into account for this paper.

DF16: Cognitive training

Figure 4 shows the derived design features together with all meta-requirements and design principles, and illustrates their relationship to each other.

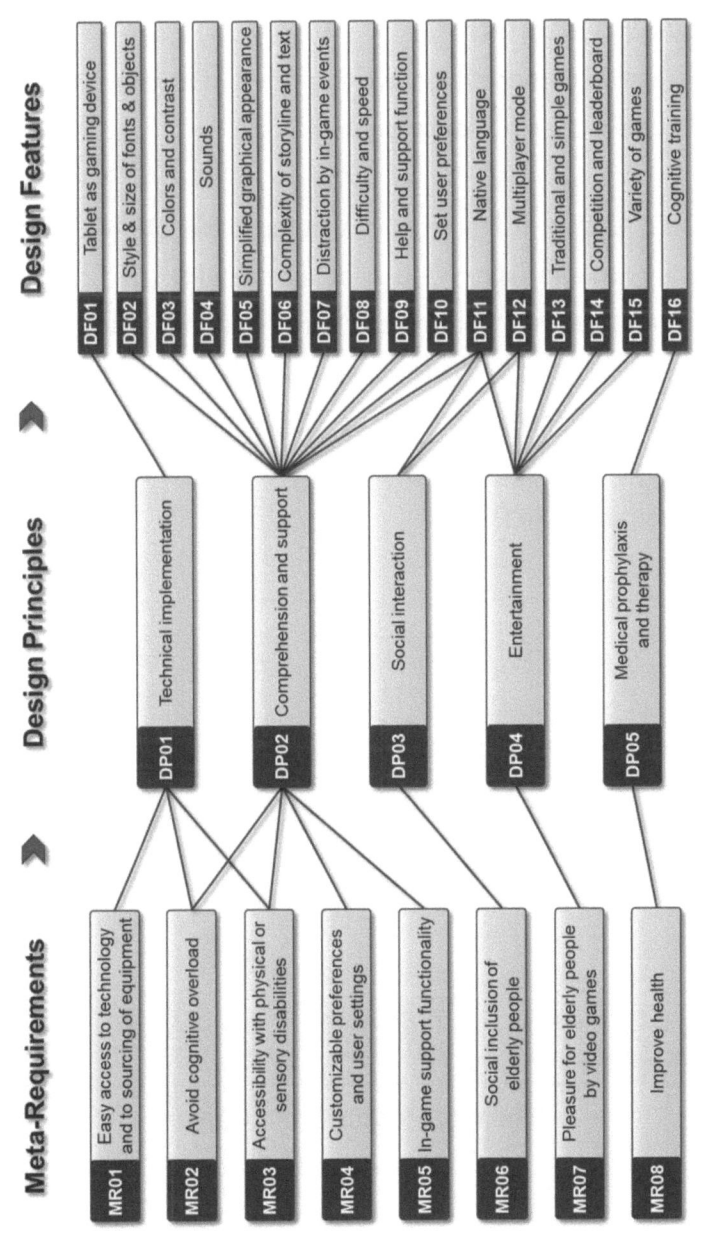

Figure 4. Meta-Requirements, Design Principles, and Design
Features

4.4 Mockup Video Games

This subsection demonstrates two examples of mockup video games and the corresponding design features.

Brain Quiz, shown in Figure 5, is a competitive (DF14), multiplayer (DF12) trivia game with video chat functionality (DF12). Cognitive skills are required by choosing the correct answer out of three for a given question (DF16). The visual appearance is simplified with sufficient space between the buttons (DF05), clear colors and contrast (DF03), large font size and large buttons (DF02), and in the user's native language (DF11).

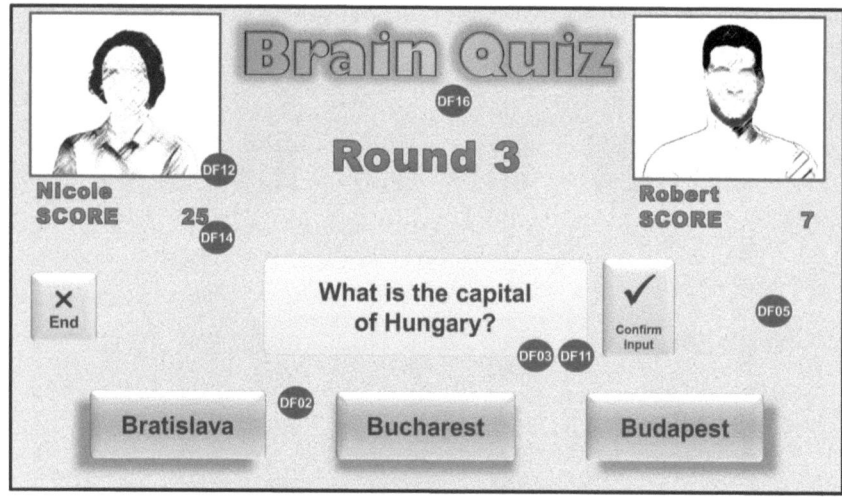

Figure 5. Mockup Trivia Game

(own drawing)

Backgammon is a traditional and strategic board game (DF13) with training of the cognitive abilities (DF16). The variant shown in Figure 6 is a single player version with the goal of winning against the computer opponent (DF14). The visualization has plain colors (DF03) with large font size and buttons (DF02). The user can set preferences (DF10) and a button with support functionality (DF09) is integrated as well.

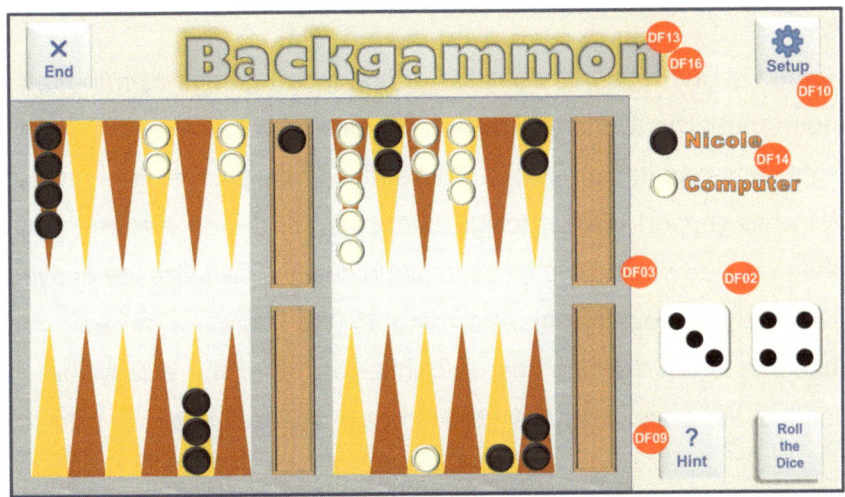

Figure 6. Mockup Board Game

(own drawing)

5 Discussion

The growing group of the elderly aged 65 and over (WHO World Health Organization, 2015) is heterogenous in their leisure demands, based on the individual development and health status of each person (Ijsselsteijn et al., 2007). There is a large body of research regarding video games for health management, but limited evaluation of playing games for entertainment purposes (Nap et al., 2009; Y.-L. Wang et al., 2020).

Guided by the research question of *how video games can be made more appealing to the elderly* and the design science methodology, eight meta-requirements have been defined from the literature review. With the support of five design principles, 16 design features have been concluded, and two mockup game designs visualize the derived guidelines as examples. According to the literature review, this research is not the first one on game design for the elderly, but in contrast to others, it is not limited to health and well-being aspects.

There are certain limitations to the research in this paper. First, the meta-requirements are derived from literature review, whereas empirical research with a test group could improve the quality of the requirements to refine the design features. Second, the steps for development and demonstration are omitted, therefore no evaluation of the artifact is possible and furthermore no iteration could be processed to improve the design features or refine the meta-requirements.

Consequently, the meta-requirements are to be refined by future empirical research, and in addition, the remaining steps of the design science methodology are for future research in order to verify and improve the artifact and specified solutions.

Furthermore, the target group of the elderly needs to be clustered, for example by age, culture, gender, or impairments, in order to derive guidelines that cover the demands of the specific subgroups to achieve the best user experience.

References

Allaire, J. C., McLaughlin, A. C., Trujillo, A., Whitlock, L. A., LaPorte, L., & Gandy, M. (2013). Successful aging through digital games: Socioemotional differences between older adult gamers and Non-gamers. *Computers in Human Behavior, 29*(4), 1302–1306. https://doi.org/10.1016/j.chb.2013.01.014

Bleakley, C. M., Charles, D., Porter-Armstrong, A., McNeill, M. D. J., McDonough, S. M., & McCormack, B. (2015). Gaming for Health: A Systematic Review of the Physical and Cognitive Effects of Interactive Computer Games in Older Adults. *Journal of Applied Gerontology, 34*(3), NP166–NP189. https://doi.org/10.1177/0733464812470747

Boot, W. R., Moxley, J. H., Roque, N. A., Andringa, R., Charness, N., Czaja, S. J., Sharit, J., Mitzner, T., Lee, C. C., & Rogers, W. A. (2018). Exploring Older Adults' Video Game Use in the PRISM Computer System. *Innovation in Aging, 2*(1), 1-13. https://doi.org/10.1093/geroni/igy009

Castilla, D., Garcia-Palacios, A., Miralles, I., Breton-Lopez, J., Parra, E., Rodriguez-Berges, S., & Botella, C. (2016). Effect of Web navigation style in elderly users. *Computers in Human Behavior, 55*, 909–920. https://doi.org/10.1016/j.chb.2015.10.034

Chua, P.-H., Jung, Y., Lwin, M. O., & Theng, Y.-L. (2013). Let's play together: Effects of video-game play on intergenerational perceptions among youth and elderly participants. *Computers in Human Behavior, 29*(6), 2303–2311. https://doi.org/10.1016/j.chb.2013.04.037

Costa, L., & Veloso, A. (2016). Being (Grand) Players: Review of Digital Games and their Potential to Enhance Intergenerational

Interactions. *Journal of Intergenerational Relationships*, *14*(1), 43–59. https://doi.org/10.1080/15350770.2016.1138273

Costa, L. V., Veloso, A. I., Loizou, M., & Arnab, S. (2018). Games for active ageing, well-being and quality of life: a pilot study. *Behaviour & Information Technology*, *37*(8), 842–854. https://doi.org/10.1080/0144929X.2018.1485744

Cota, T. T., Ishitani, L., & Vieira, N. (2015). Mobile game design for the elderly: A study with focus on the motivation to play. *Computers in Human Behavior*, *51*, 96–105. https://doi.org/10.1016/j.chb.2015.04.026

Czaja, S. J., & Lee, C. C. (2007). The impact of aging on access to technology. *Universal Access in the Information Society*, *5*(4), 341–349. https://doi.org/10.1007/s10209-006-0060-x

Czaja, S. J., & Lee, C. C. (2012). Older Adults and Information Technology: Opportunities and Challenges. In J. A. Jacko (Ed.), *The Human–Computer Interaction Handbook: Fundamentals, Evolving Technologies, and Emerging Applications* (3rd ed., pp. 825–840). CRC Press.

Derboven, J., van Gils, M., & Grooff, D. de (2012). Designing for collaboration: a study in intergenerational social game design. *Universal Access in the Information Society*, *11*(1), 57–65. https://doi.org/10.1007/s10209-011-0233-0

Dickinson, A., Newell, A. F., Smith, M. J., & Hill, R. L. (2005). Introducing the Internet to the over-60s: Developing an email system for older novice computer users. *Interacting with Computers*, *17*(6), 621–642. https://doi.org/10.1016/j.intcom.2005.09.003

Gamberini, L., Alcaniz, M., Barresi, G., Fabregat, M., Prontu, L., & Seraglia, B. (2008). Playing for a real bonus: Videogames to empower elderly people. *Journal of Cyber Therapy and Rehabilitation, 1*(1), 37–48.

Gerling, K. M., Schulte, F. P., Smeddinck, J., & Masuch, M. (2012). Game Design for Older Adults: Effects of Age-Related Changes on Structural Elements of Digital Games. In M. Herrlich, R. Malaka, & M. Masuch (Eds.), *Lecture notes in computer science. Entertainment Computing - ICEC 2012: 11th International Conference, ICEC 2012* (Vol. 7522, pp. 235–242). Springer Berlin Heidelberg. https://doi.org/10.1007/978-3-642-33542-6_20

Gregor, S., & Hevner, A. R. (2013). Positioning and Presenting Design Science Research for Maximum Impact. *MIS Quarterly, 37*(2), 337–355. https://doi.org/10.25300/MISQ/2013/37.2.01

Hanson, V. L., & Crayne, S. (2005). Personalization of Web browsing: adaptations to meet the needs of older adults. *Universal Access in the Information Society, 4*(1), 46–58. https://doi.org/10.1007/s10209-005-0110-9

Hawthorn, D. (2000). Possible implications of aging for interface designers. *Interacting with Computers, 12*(5), 507–528. https://doi.org/10.1016/S0953-5438(99)00021-1

Hevner, A. R., March, S. T., Park, J., & Ram, S. (2004). Design Science in Information Systems Research. *MIS Quarterly, 28*(1), 75-105. https://doi.org/10.2307/25148625

Ijsselsteijn, W. A., Nap, H. H., Kort, Y. A. W. de, & Poels, K. (2007). Digital game design for elderly users. In B. Kapralos,

M. Katchabaw, & J. Rajnovich (Eds.), *Proceedings of the 2007 conference on Future Play* (pp. 17–22). ACM Press. https://doi.org/10.1145/1328202.1328206

Jochems, N., Vetter, S., & Schlick, C. (2013). A comparative study of information input devices for aging computer users. *Behaviour & Information Technology, 32*(9), 902–919. https://doi.org/10.1080/0144929X.2012.692100

Li, S.-C., Lindenberger, U., & Sikström, S. (2001). Aging cognition: From neuromodulation to representation. *Trends in Cognitive Sciences, 5*(11), 479–486. https://doi.org/10.1016/S1364-6613(00)01769-1

Lukaitis, A., & Davey, B. (2012). Web Design for Mature-Aged Travellers: Readability as a Design Issue. *Journal of Marketing Development and Competitiveness, 6*(2), 69–80.

Meth, H., Mueller, B., & Maedche, A. (2015). Designing a Requirement Mining System. *Journal of the Association for Information Systems, 16*(9), 799–837. https://doi.org/10.17705/1jais.00408

Nap, H. H., Kort, Y. A. W. de, & Ijsselsteijn, W. A. (2009). Senior gamers: Preferences, motivations and needs. *Gerontechnology, 8*(4), 247–262. https://doi.org/10.4017/gt.2009.08.04.003.00

Nguyen, H. T. T., Ishmatova, D., Tapanainen, T., Liukkonen, T. N., Katajapuu, N., Makila, T., & Luimula, M. (2017). Impact of Serious Games on Health and Well-being of Elderly: A Systematic Review. *Proceedings of the Hawaii International Conference on System Sciences*, 3695–3704. https://doi.org/10.24251/HICSS.2017.447

Orimo, H., Ito, H., Suzuki, T., Araki, A., Hosoi, T., & Sawabe, M. (2006). Reviewing the definition of "elderly". *Geriatrics and Gerontology International,* 6(3), 149–158. https://doi.org/10.1111/j.1447-0594.2006.00341.x

Palacio, R. R., Acosta, C. O., Cortez, J., & Morán, A. L. (2017). Usability perception of different video game devices in elderly users. *Universal Access in the Information Society, 16*(1), 103–113. https://doi.org/10.1007/s10209-015-0435-y

Peffers, K., Tuunanen, T., Rothenberger, M. A., & Chatterjee, S. (2007). A Design Science Research Methodology for Information Systems Research. *Journal of Management Information Systems, 24*(3), 45–77. https://doi.org/10.2753/MIS0742-1222240302

Salthouse, T. A. (1996). The Processing-Speed Theory of Adult Age Differences in Cognition. *Psychological Review, 103*(3), 403–428. https://doi.org/10.1037/0033-295X.103.3.403

United Nations. (2020). *World Population Ageing 2019 (ST/ESA/SER.A/444).* https://www.un.org/en/development/desa/population/publications/pdf/ageing/WorldPopulationAgeing2019-Report.pdf

Vasconcelos, A., Silva, P. A., Caseiro, J., Nunes, F., & Teixeira, L. F. (2012). Designing tablet-based games for seniors: the example of CogniPlay, a cognitive gaming platform. In K. Isbister, F. Mueller, & R. Bernhaupt (Eds.), *Proceedings of the 4th International Conference on Fun and Games* (pp. 1–10). ACM. https://doi.org/10.1145/2367616.2367617

Walls, J. G., Widmeyer, G. R., & El Sawy, O. A. (1992). Building an Information System Design Theory for Vigilant EIS. *Information Systems Research*, 3(1), 36–59. https://doi.org/10.1287/isre.3.1.36

Wang, J.-Y. (2014). Comparison of game experience and preferences between young and elderly. In *2014 International Conference on Audio, Language and Image Processing* (pp. 101–105). IEEE. https://doi.org/10.1109/ICALIP.2014.7009765

Wang, Y.-L., Hou, H.-T., & Tsai, C.-C. (2020). A systematic literature review of the impacts of digital games designed for older adults. *Educational Gerontology*, 46(1), 1–17. https://doi.org/10.1080/03601277.2019.1694448

Whitlock, L. A., McLaughlin, A. C., & Allaire, J. C. (2012). Individual differences in response to cognitive training: Using a multi-modal, attentionally demanding game-based intervention for older adults. *Computers in Human Behavior*, 28(4), 1091–1096. https://doi.org/10.1016/j.chb.2012.01.012

WHO World Health Organization. (2015). *World report on ageing and health*. WHO Press.

Zaphiris, P., Kurniawan, S., & Ghiawadwala, M. (2007). A systematic approach to the development of research-based web design guidelines for older people. *Universal Access in the Information Society*, 6(1), 59–75. https://doi.org/10.1007/s10209-006-0054-8

Zelinski, E. M., & Reyes, R. (2009). Cognitive benefits of computer games for older adults. *Gerontechnology*, 8(4), 220–235. https://doi.org/10.4017/gt.2009.08.04.004.00

YOUR KNOWLEDGE HAS VALUE

- We will publish your bachelor's and
  master's thesis, essays and papers

- Your own eBook and book -
  sold worldwide in all relevant shops

- Earn money with each sale

Upload your text at www.GRIN.com
and publish for free